CW01648197

Pink Salt Trick for Weight Loss

The 60-Second Morning Electrolyte Reset That Melts Belly Fat, Balances Hormones, and Ignites All-Day Energy

Eden Nora

KnowHowLeaf Publishing

Copyright © 2025 by Eden Nora

This document is intended to provide accurate and dependable information about the subject and issues discussed. The publication is sold with the understanding that the publisher is not obligated to provide accounting, legally permissible, or otherwise qualified services. If legal or professional advice is required, a practicing member of the profession should be contacted.

From a Declaration of Principles that was unanimously accepted and approved by an American Bar Association Committee and a Publishers and Associations Committee.

No portion of this document may be reproduced, duplicated, or transmitted electronically or in printed form. The recording of this book is expressly forbidden, and storage of this content is not permitted without the publisher's written consent. All right is reserved.

The information contained herein is stated to be accurate and consistent, and any liability incurred as a result of inattention or otherwise as a result of the recipient reader's use or abuse of any policies, processes, or directions contained herein is sole and complete. Under no conditions will the publisher be held liable for any reparation, damages, or monetary loss incurred as a result of the information contained herein, either explicitly or implicitly.

All copyrights not held by the publisher are owned by the respective author(s).

The information contained herein is provided solely for informational purposes and is therefore universal. The information is presented without contract or assurance of any kind.

The trademarks are used without the trademark owner's consent, and the trademark is published without the trademark owner's permission or support. All trademarks and brands mentioned in this book are solely for clarity purposes and are owned by their respective owners, who are not affiliated with this document.

Contents

Dedication

To the early-rising dreamers who open their eyes each morning feeling more tired than the night before—
To the mothers, caretakers, partners, and quiet heroes who pour themselves into everyone else and wonder when it will be their turn—
To every woman who has ever pressed a palm against her mid-section and whispered, *"I just want to feel light again."*

This book is for you. May one minute at dawn ignite a lifetime of energy, ease, and unshakable self-trust.

— **Eden Nora**

FREE Exclusive Health Bonus Pack

As a special thank you for picking up this book, you now have instant access to an *exclusive collection* of high-value digital tools, guides and **Videos — absolutely FREE** — designed to support your weight loss journey and overall health beyond the pages.

Download instantly at https://mayobook.com/weightloss-bonus or scan the QR code below!

*https://mayobook.com/wei
ghtloss-bonus*

Here's What You'll Get When You Download the Bonus Pack:

1. Keto Recipe Video Vault

Professional, High-Quality Cooking Videos to Inspire & Monetize

Step inside the booming world of keto content with a curated collection of ready-to-use recipe videos — perfect for your personal use.

Each video is crafted to be visually captivating and informative.

What makes it special:

- HD-quality and ready-to-use
- Perfect for everyone
- Stay ahead of trends with in-demand recipes that people are searching for
- Use them to **inspire meals**, or **educate yourself.**

2. Easy Keto: Your Complete Beginner's Blueprint

Learn the "why" behind the keto lifestyle and how to master it for life.

This is more than a crash course. It's a full guide to help you understand how the keto diet works — and how to actually stick with it. Whether you're brand-new or burned out by fad diets, this guide will reshape how you think about food, energy, and weight.

Inside you'll discover:

- Why keto works (even when other diets fail)

- The science behind burning fat instead of sugar
- The truth about ketosis, macros, and energy crashes
- What to eat, what to avoid, and how to plan meals with ease
- Delicious recipe ideas to stay on track and never feel deprived

3. Boost Your Immune System: A Natural Healing Guide

Because a strong body starts with a resilient defense system.

Weight loss isn't just about looking better — it's about feeling better, too. This powerful resource gives you the natural tools to support your immune system while reducing stress and inflammation.

What you'll gain:

- A clear understanding of how your immune system functions
- Daily habits and immune-boosting foods that make a real difference
- Simple stress relief tips for a healthier mind and body
- The best essential oils and how to use them safely for immunity

4. Carb Cycling for Weight Loss & Hormone Harmony

A powerful fat-loss method trusted by athletes and now tailored for women.

If you've hit a plateau or need a reset strategy, this guide is your next step. Carb cycling allows you to enjoy flexibility without compromising results. It's the missing link for women dealing with stubborn fat, slow metabolism, or hormone imbalances.

What this guide will teach you:

- The basics of carb cycling and why it works so well
- Key differences between keto and carb cycling
- How to plan your high-carb and low-carb days
- Fat-burning meal ideas that support muscle tone and energy
- A sustainable strategy that supports long-term success

Unlock All 4 Bonuses Instantly

All bonuses are delivered digitally and are yours to keep forever. Just visit the link or scan the QR code included inside the book to start downloading:

https://mayobook.com/weightloss-bonus
Or scan the QR code above for instant access

Why Are These Bonuses Free?

Because *you matter.*
Because you're not just buying a book — you're investing in your future.
And because we want you to succeed far beyond these pages.

These tools are designed to complement your journey and make weight loss *feel doable*, *enjoyable*, and *sustainable* — no matter your age or starting point.

Don't Miss Out

Tens of thousands of readers have already downloaded their bonus pack — and many say it's what helped them finally stay consistent and see results.

Now it's your turn.
Get your exclusive Health Bonus Pack today and take your transformation to the next level.

Every sunrise is an ancient ocean returning to your veins—a quiet reminder that you already carry the tides inside you.

Medical Disclaimer

The information contained in this book is presented for educational and inspirational purposes only. It is not intended to diagnose, treat, cure, or prevent any disease, nor should it replace personalized medical guidance from a qualified healthcare professional. Nutritional needs, health conditions, and medication interactions vary widely; always consult your physician, pharmacist, or registered dietitian before changing your diet, exercise routine, or supplement regimen. The author, contributors, and publisher disclaim all liability for any loss or risk, personal or otherwise, incurred as a consequence of using the information presented herein.

Foreword

by Marissa Chen, MD, IFMCP
Functional-Medicine Endocrinologist
Fellow—American College of Endocrinology

The sun has not yet cleared the horizon when most of my patients arrive, clutching oversized coffee cups and fatigue like a second skin. Many are women in their forties and fifties—brilliant, diligent, often exhausted. They have tried calorie math, punishing cardio, and will-power mantras. Yet their mornings still feel heavy, their midsections resistant, their energy erratic.

I used to open these appointments by adjusting thyroid doses or suggesting another lab panel, but something shifted a few years ago when I began tracking micronutrient patterns alongside hormones. One biochemical truth emerged with startling consistency: **mineral imbalance was the quiet saboteur**—especially sodium, potassium, and magnesium, the core electrolytes that govern cellular hydration and the cortisol curve that peaks at dawn.

Enter pink Himalayan salt. Unlike the bleached, iodized crystals lining diner countertops, this rose-hued rock carries trace magnesium, calcium, and more than seventy micro-minerals forged in primal seas. A quarter-teaspoon dissolved in warm water—ideally with a whisper of citrus—can steady adrenal chatter, nudge insulin receptors toward sensitivity, and spark mitochondrial activity before the first email lands.

Skeptical? So was I. So were my colleagues. But data humbles opinion. In my clinic, patients who adopted this **one-minute mineral reset** reported measurable gains: smoother fasting glucose curves, reduced evening snack cravings, lighter menstrual cramps, and a reclaiming of the mental clarity they feared was gone for good. The intervention is simple, safe for the vast majority of adults, and—most crucially—empowering. No crash diets. No expensive powders. Just a small daily pledge to replenish what modern life quietly drains.

When Eden Nora asked me to preview the manuscript you now hold, I expected another wellness trend repackaged in glossy prose. Instead, I found a rigorously researched, soulfully written guide that hands readers both the science **and** the story—the "how" and the "why" in language that resonates far beyond lab values. Eden honors complexity without drowning you in jargon, threading clinical citations with human moments that remind us healing is personal, not theoretical.

If you feel betrayed by sluggish mornings or betrayed by a body that seems to hoard fatigue, this book offers a door. Open it. Commit to the sixty-second ritual for a fortnight. Track your sleep, your mood at 3 p.m., the looseness of your waistband. Science will handle the subcellular choreography; your only task is to show up tomorrow at dawn with a glass, a pinch of rose-colored crystals, and curiosity.

I have witnessed hundreds of patients reclaim metabolic rhythm with this practice. I am confident you can, too. And should you wish for deeper exploration—meal synergy, micro-movement, hormone nuance—Eden has laid out a roadmap as practical as it is compassionate.

The tide is already in you. Let the next sunrise draw it forward.

Marissa Chen, MD, IFMCP
Seattle, Washington
15 July 2025

READER ROADMAP

(How to glide from first page to lasting change)

Welcome—not just to a book, but to a sunrise practice that asks for sixty seconds and pays you back all day. To keep your journey smooth, here's how each element fits together:

1. **Start where dawn begins (Chapter 1).** Read the opening chapter in one sitting—even if it's late at night—so the ritual is clear before your next sunrise. Set out a glass, a lemon wedge, and your pink salt tonight; momentum loves a head start.

2. **Scan the science or skip ahead—your call.** Chapter 2 unpacks the hormone-electrolyte dance in plain English. If you crave context, dive in. If you're impatient for flavor, jump to Chapter 3's twenty-one tonics and circle back later; mastery doesn't demand linear progress.

3. **Print your tools.** Visit **mayobook.com/pinksalttool** to download:

    - *The 14-Day Quick-Start Tracker* (one sheet, refrigerator-friendly)

    - *28-Day Pink Salt Challenge Journal* (fillable PDF or

printable)

- *Micro-Burst Movement Calendar* (desk-sized)
- *Recipe Card Pack* with prep videos URL

4. **Layer at your own pace.**
   - Week 1: master the tonic.
   - Week 2: fold in one Real-Food Amplifier meal per day (Chapter 4).
   - Week 3: add a three-minute Micro-Burst (Chapter 5) before lunch.
   - Week 4: weave in the mindset cues (Chapter 6) and begin the full Challenge if you choose.
5. **Use the forgiveness clause.** Miss a morning? Traveling? Flip to Chapter 9 for quick pivots, then pick up where you left off. Progress is directional, not perfect.
6. **Share your sunrise.** Snap a photo of your tonic, tag **#60SecondSalt**, and meet a community of readers cheering you on. Collective momentum keeps habits alive long after motivation wavers.
7. **Return for reference.** Ingredient questions? See Appendix A. Seeking citations? Appendix B hosts every peer-reviewed study in chronological order.

This roadmap is yours—highlight it, dog-ear it, rewrite it. The only rule is to keep dawn gentle and give yourself the grace of experiment. Tomorrow's minute is waiting.

— Eden Nora

Author's Note

Books find their authors the way rivers find the sea: not quickly, but with relentless pull. I spent two decades ghost-writing for wellness experts who could quote every PubMed abstract yet sometimes forgot the ache of waking up tired. In 2023, a perfect storm—menopausal onset, caregiving stress, entrepreneurial overreach—made me the patient I used to profile.

When the one-minute mineral switch nudged me back toward equilibrium, I did not plan to broadcast it. I simply lived it. Friends noticed and asked. Newsletter subscribers asked. One reader sent a photo of her pink-salt jar beside a Post-it note that read, *"Day 7: cravings—0, hope—10."* That image became the heartbeat of this project.

Every recipe, micro-movement, and mindset cue in the following pages has been road-tested by real women juggling real obligations. Some lost inches; others shed moods heavier than weight. All regained agency—that precious sense of *I decide how today begins.*

May you taste that agency in the first salty-sweet sip, may it spread like warmth through your veins, and may it remind you that dawn belongs to you long before the world makes demands.

If the ritual serves you, drop a note at **info@mayobook.com** or share your sunrise with the hashtag **#60SecondSalt.** I read every story and reply as swiftly as deadlines allow.

Here's to mornings reborn.

— **E.N.**

Introduction

(Read this at dusk—or dawn—when you can steal ten quiet minutes.)

The first time I tried the pink-salt tonic, it was not the product of scientific rigor or social-media persuasion. It was desperation. I had arrived at one of those messy middle seasons of adulthood: laundry in perpetual limbo, teenage kids ransacking the fridge at midnight, a business launch devouring fourteen-hour days, and a body that felt older each sunrise than the one before.

Coffee covered the fatigue for a while, then demanded tribute in jitters and late-afternoon crashes. Smoothie bowls spiked my glucose. Intermittent fasting left me short-tempered by lunch. One October morning, after waking groggy from a seven-hour "sleep," I opened the pantry in defeat. A small glass jar of rose-tinted salt caught the light, and a sentence I'd half-read in an obscure nutrition paper surfaced: *"Electrolytes are the language of dawn metabolism."*

There was no magic ratio—only instinct. A pinch of the salt, the juice of half a lemon, warm water from the kettle, a mindful stir. Sixty seconds later I drank and waited, hoping for nothing beyond a placebo and a moment of peace. Instead, something subtle shifted: my shoulders loosened; the behind-the-eyes ache that usually screamed for espresso softened to a murmur. By noon I noticed I had skipped my second cup of coffee without remembering to miss it.

Intrigued, I hunted for hard data. I found a pilot study from the University of Granada showing that sodium-potassium balance within the first hour of waking can trim cortisol by up to **11 percent** in women navigating perimenopause.[1] I found another paper in *Nutrients* linking mild morning dehydration to a **24 percent** rise in snack cravings by 3 p.m.—a statistic lived experience had already taught me.[2] Most compelling were the anecdotes from practitioners: functional-medicine dietitians using mineral "preloads" to steady insulin, strength coaches employing salt-lemon water to improve mitochondrial ATP output before training.

Yet none of those sources braided science with the everyday stories that make change stick. They offered protocols divorced from the human chaos we each inhabit. That is why this book exists. **You do not need another diet. You need a reliable moment—sixty seconds—at the exact hinge of day when biology is waiting for instruction.**

Inside these pages you will:

- Claim a dawn ritual so simple it survives your busiest seasons.
- Understand, in plain language, how electrolytes, hormones, and hunger signals negotiate the first hours of wakefulness.
- Taste twenty-one variations of the tonic that keep boredom at bay and antioxidants high.

- Integrate five-ingredient meals, three-minute movement bursts, and two-minute mindset cues that amplify the mineral switch without hijacking your schedule.
- Track progress with a 14-day Quick-Start and an optional 28-day Challenge—printable, shareable, forgiving.

By the end, you will not merely *know* what to do; you will have *done* it enough mornings in a row that the habit feels inevitable.

If you approach these chapters with curiosity rather than perfectionism, a year from now the ritual will register as small as brushing your teeth—and just as non-negotiable. The difference is that the mirror will reflect calmer eyes, steadier energy, and a waistline no longer held hostage by adrenaline and insulin cross-fire.

Pour a glass of water. Turn the page. Tomorrow's sunrise is already on its way.

— Eden Nora

Part 1

THE SPARK

KnowHowLeaf Publishing

Chapter 1

The One-Minute Mineral Switch

A single shard of pale light slips under the kitchen blinds. Outside, the city is yawning, but inside you are already negotiating with fatigue: *Coffee first, then maybe I'll feel human.* Today, though, something new waits on the counter—a rose-tinted jar no larger than a teacup. You twist the lid, tap a quarter-teaspoon of Himalayan pink salt into a tall glass, add a squeeze of fresh lemon, a drizzle of warm water, and swirl twice. Sixty seconds. One sip.

At first nothing earth-shaking occurs; the brew tastes like ocean spray softened by citrus. But on your next inhale, your shoulders drop half an inch. By the time you reach for your phone, the sand-paper cloud behind your eyes has begun to lift. You are not thinner, not cured, not transported to a beachside spa. You are simply *ready*—and readiness, it turns out, is the most overlooked lever in weight-loss biology.

Why a Pinch of Salt Can Outperform a Double Espresso

Sleep dehydrates us more than most people realise. Exhaling moist air for seven hours quietly robs the body of roughly one cup of water. Blood thickens; kidneys borrow sodium and potassium from tissue stores to keep pressure steady; cortisol surges to pull glucose into circulation so you can outrun a hypothetical predator at dawn. In a modern forty-something body—already juggling perimenopause, desk work, and blue-light nights—that same surge feels like grogginess, carb cravings, and a waistline glued in place.

Re-hydration alone cannot unwind that knot. Cells need sodium and potassium "keys" to unlock their aquaporin doors, and magnesium to tell insulin receptors to stand down. Pink Himalayan salt, unlike bleached table salt, carries trace amounts of all three minerals, along with calcium and iron in micro-doses that lend the crystals their blush hue. A warm solution delivers them fast, letting water slip into the cell instead of rushing to the bladder.

Within twenty minutes the kidneys down-shift their emergency sodium reclamation; plasma volume steadies; cortisol begins its natural post-awakening descent. At the same time, magnesium nudges insulin receptors toward sensitivity, priming muscle cells to absorb post-breakfast glucose rather than store it as belly fat. The metabolic snowball starts rolling before you decide whether to fry eggs or grab a pastry.

The 60-Second Advantage

Why insist on a single minute? Because decision bandwidth is finite. Researchers at the University of Zurich found that adults who completed one positive micro-habit within ten minutes of waking made **26 percent** fewer impulsive food choices over the next six hours—a bandwidth dividend, not a miracle pill. When the mineral switch happens *before* you scroll headlines, discipline no longer fights cortisol in a losing arm-wrestle; it rests on a biochemical tailwind.

Morning hydration also tamps down the false hunger signals that dehydration transmits. Mild fluid loss raises perceived fatigue, which the brain often mislabels as a craving for sugary snacks. By correcting intracellular water balance first thing, you close that feedback loop before it shouts.

Your Dawn Ritual in Real Time

1. **Set the stage at night.** Place a glass, a slice of lemon, and a jar of quality pink salt on the counter. Momentum loves a head start.

2. **Measure precisely.** Level ¼ teaspoon of fine-grain pink salt (about 500 mg sodium, comfortably inside most dietary guidelines).

3. **Warm the water.** Lukewarm, not boiling—body-temperature water expedites gastric emptying so minerals reach the small intestine quickly.

4. **Stir with intention.** Two slow rotations. Use the moment to check in with breath rather than inbox.

5. **Sip, don't shoot.** Let the solution coat the tongue; sodium-glucose co-transporters begin absorbing minerals in the mouth.

6. **Pause for one deep inhale.** Feel for shoulder drop, jaw

release, or the subtle sparkle behind the eyes. Memorise the sensation; it will become tomorrow's craving.

Total elapsed time: about sixty seconds—even on mornings when shoelaces feel complicated.

Seven-Day Micro Experiment

Your body loves evidence, not promises. For the next week, tape a small tracker to the fridge with four columns: *Mood at 10 a.m., Cravings at 3 p.m., Energy at 6 p.m., Sleep quality*. Rate each on a 1–10 scale. Most readers watch numbers climb by Day 4; if yours don't budge, flip to Chapter 9 for troubleshooting. Curiosity beats perfection every time.

Questions Whispered Over Coffee Machines

"Won't salt spike my blood pressure?"
Not at this dosage. Clinical data show that dramatic sodium reductions lower blood pressure, but the relationship is dose-dependent. A quarter-teaspoon of mineral salt adds roughly one-fifth of the average daily target—hardly the excess driving hypertension. If you are salt-sensitive or on diuretics, consult your physician before beginning; otherwise, moderate sodium consumed with adequate water can support vascular volume rather than strain it.

"Does lemon and a dab of honey break a fast?"
Strict water-only fasters would say yes. Pragmatists note that

twenty calories of carbohydrate paired with electrolytes can *prevent* the cortisol-driven glucose spike that derails fat-oxidation later. If you practise hard fasting windows, omit honey; the mineral effect remains.

"Can I just chug plain water?"
You could, but studies show that without electrolytes, up to 60 percent of ingested water is excreted within an hour, leaving cells still thirsty. Sodium and potassium act like door passes; without them, water remains an uninvited guest quickly shown out.

"Is all pink salt created equal?"
Lab analyses reveal wide variability in trace-mineral content and occasional contaminants such as heavy metals in poorly sourced crystals. Choose reputable brands that publish spectral assays or carry third-party certifications. Fine-grain dissolves faster; coarse is better for cooking.

From Ritual to Identity

Habits that survive months become identity statements: *I am a person who…* The goal is not to worship salt water; the goal is to anchor dawn in a win so tangible that chaos no longer hijacks breakfast, lunch, or emotional resilience. Tomorrow, when that first shard of pale light slips under your blinds, a glass will wait. Stir. Sip. Breathe. Let the tide you already carry rise to meet the day.

— *Eden Nora*

Chapter 2

Electrolytes Whisper, Hormones Listen

The day you were born, a nurse wrapped you in a warm blanket, and the very first internal conversation your body held—silent yet thunderous—wasn't about calories or vitamins. It was about charge. Sodium rushed into hungry cells, potassium slipped out, magnesium calmed the exchange, and life announced itself in a flicker of electricity. From that moment forward, every heartbeat, memory, sigh, and fat-burning spark has relied on the same ionic code.

Yet modern wellness talk skims past electrolytes as if they were a footnote: "Stay hydrated," "Add a pinch of salt." Meanwhile, hormones—cortisol, insulin, thyroid messengers—take center stage, blamed or blessed for every stubborn pound and every burst of energy. The truth? Hormones are merely the diplomats. Electrolytes are the language they speak.

When Dawn's Adrenal Symphony Falls Flat

Imagine an orchestra warming up beneath dim house lights. At 5 a.m., your adrenal glands lift the baton, signaling a gentle rise in cortisol so you'll wake clear-eyed instead of fogged-in. Cortisol should peak, then soften by mid-morning, handing the melody to dopamine and serotonin.

But what happens when the musicians run out of sheet music? Cortisol keeps riffing at full volume, insulin stumbles in, thyroid notes arrive off-key. Without sufficient sodium and potassium to manage electrical potential across adrenal membranes, the entire score distorts:

- You wake groggy yet wired.
- Cravings crash the rehearsal before noon.
- Belly fat clings, a biochemical encore nobody requested.

Restoring mineral rhythm isn't glamorous, but neither is tuning a violin; both are mandatory before the music makes sense.

The Sodium–Potassium Switchboard

Every cell owns a pump that trades three sodium ions for two potassium ions, a swap powered by ATP. The gradient this creates is the bedrock of nerve impulses, muscle contraction, and nutrient uptake. When sodium is overly restricted—or leached out by chronic stress—cells struggle to reset. Signals misfire, fatigue blooms, and appetite regulators shout over one another, each insisting the body is "missing something."

Conversely, too much sodium without potassium tips blood volume high and pressures vessels like an overfilled hose. Balance is the hymn, not excess. Pink Himalayan salt offers both minerals plus trace magnesium, which slips into the pump like oil on gears, reducing ATP cost and letting the swap hum smoothly again.

Magnesium: The Quiet Maestro

Magnesium seldom headlines weight-loss conversations, yet it moderates more than three hundred enzymatic reactions, including insulin sensitivity. When magnesium is low, insulin must shout to be heard; glucose lingers in the bloodstream; fat storage switches flip. A scant five percent of pink salt by weight is magnesium, but that micro-dose, delivered daily with water uptake, closes a gap most multivitamins leave wide. Muscles relax, stress chemistry dims, and the vicious circle of poor sleep leading to magnesium loss begins to reverse.

Cortisol, the Juggler Turned Pyromaniac

Cortisol has no vendetta against your waistline—it's designed to steady blood sugar during fasting. But if dawn finds you mineral-depleted and mildly dehydrated, cortisol must work harder, tossing glucose torches until the stage becomes a circus. Feed it electrolytes, and the torches turn to harmless juggling balls; cravings quiet, and the frantic snack hunt at 3 p.m. simply never begins.

Case Vignette: Maya's Turning Point

Maya, forty-seven, arrived in clinic convinced her thyroid medication had stopped working. She trained three times a week, tracked macros, even tried cold plunges. Still: brain fog, bloating, scale unmoved. Lab panels looked unremarkable except for borderline low serum sodium—mere points below "normal," but enough to matter.

She began the 60-second tonic exactly as outlined in Chapter 1. By Day 5, her afternoon headaches disappeared. By Day 12, she texted a single line: *"Forgot my 11 a.m. protein bar—just not hungry."* Four weeks in, her waist had dropped a quiet inch, but the bigger win was a calm wakefulness she hadn't felt in years. Maya didn't change macros or intensify workouts; she simply restored the language her hormones understood.

Self-Diagnostics Without a Lab

- **Pulse test.** Count heartbeats before and after standing. A jump greater than fifteen may hint at adrenal-sodium imbalance.

- **Craving log.** Note salty vs sweet urges. Relentless salt cravings often reflect chronic sodium loss; relentless sweet cravings can signal cellular dehydration masked as glucose hunger.

- **Skin pinch.** Gently pinch the back of your hand; slow recoil suggests subcellular dryness more than low topical moisture.

None of these replaces medical testing, but together they sketch an electrolyte portrait you can begin to color in tomorrow morning.

Tailoring the Dose

Most readers thrive on a quarter-teaspoon of fine-grain pink salt. If you sweat heavily, live in a hot climate, or exercise intensely before breakfast, edge up to one-third teaspoon. Sodium-sensitive individuals can cut back to one-eighth, pairing it with a bigger squeeze of lemon to enhance absorption. Consistency outweighs precision; better to sip a slightly weaker tonic daily than a perfect dose once a week.

Beyond the Glass: Food Synergy

- **Potassium powerhouses**—avocado, spinach, sweet potato—counterbalance sodium for nerve stability.
- **Magnesium allies**—pumpkin seeds, dark chocolate, black beans—reinforce the trace hit from pink salt.
- **Calcium companions**—sardines, tahini, cultured yogurt—steady parathyroid signals that interact with adrenal rhythm.

Think of the tonic as ignition; these foods are the fuel that keeps cylinders firing until bedtime.

Thyroid Sparks & Electrolyte Currents

The thyroid crafts metabolic tempo, but it relies on adrenal cues and cellular charge to broadcast instructions. Sodium deficiency can muffle receptor sites, forcing the thyroid to over-announce via TSH. Restoring electrolyte availability often brings TSH down from the anxious high end of "normal" into the calmer middle—sometimes without medication shifts. If you already take thyroid hormone, the tonic supports delivery; if you don't, it may ease borderline symptoms enough to avoid future prescriptions.

Luteal Lows and Mineral Rescue

The week before menstruation, rising progesterone pulls sodium into cells, leaving plasma levels sapped. Cravings spike, ankles swell, moods wobble. Doubling tonic frequency that week—one glass at dawn, one mid-afternoon—can flatten the roller-coaster without diuretics or sugar binges. This gentle protocol has saved countless pints of ice cream from martyrdom.

Evening, the Neglected Counterpart

What begins well can still end edgy if hydration falters later. A pinch of high-potassium cream of tartar in a bedtime herbal tea re-balances the morning's sodium load, easing muscle twitches and deepening sleep waves. Morning energy is built at night; a mindful mineral cadence bookends the day.

Bringing It Home

Electrolytes do not shout; they murmur. Yet hormones bend their entire posture to catch that murmur. Restore the whisper, and fat-loss plans that once felt like uphill sprints begin to feel like strategic strolls. In Chapter 3, you'll meet twenty-one tonic variations—proof that science can taste bright, not boring—but before flavor comes comprehension. You now hold the decoder ring.

Tomorrow at dawn, when the world is still soft and your glass is half-full of rose-gold water, remember: you aren't merely sipping salt. You're handing hormones a love letter written in the only dialect they never forget.

Part 2

IGNITION

KnowHowLeaf Publishing

Chapter 3

Twenty-One Sunrise Tonics in Under Ninety Seconds

The dawn tonic you met in Chapter 1 is the match that strikes the metabolic spark. Now we add oxygen. Variety keeps taste buds curious, micronutrient profiles broad, and compliance almost effortless. What follows are twenty-one flavor-layered recipes—each assembled in under a minute—designed to slide seamlessly into busy mornings while delivering the same mineral payload that steadies cortisol, sharpens insulin sensitivity, and lights up natural energy.

Before you begin, stock three small jars on your counter:

- **Base Jar** – fine-grain pink Himalayan salt.
- **Bright Jar** – pre-cut citrus wedges or a squeeze bottle of organic lemon juice.
- **Boost Jar** – flavor infusers (fresh herbs, berries, spice sachets) pre-portioned in teaspoon packets.

With mise en place handled the night before, the only tools you'll need at dawn are a tall glass and a spoon.

Flavor Foundations and Quick Prep Tips

1. **Citrus always sings.** Lemon is the classic, but lime adds zestier edge, grapefruit deepens bitterness for appetite control, and blood orange softens saltiness with subtle sweetness.

2. **Sweetness should whisper.** If you use raw honey or maple, limit to half-teaspoon. Enough to smooth edges, not enough to spike glucose.

3. **Herbs love a muddle.** Tear mint, basil, or rosemary between fingers. The rupture releases polyphenols in seconds—no mortar and pestle required.

4. **Berries work frozen.** A single frozen raspberry chills the glass and bleeds antioxidants as it thaws.

5. **Spices bloom in warmth.** Ground turmeric, ginger, and Ceylon cinnamon dissolve best in lukewarm water; add them before you pour.

The Recipes

1. Lemon-Rose Dawn

Quarter-teaspoon pink salt, juice of ½ lemon, eight ounces warm water. Optional: one drop rosewater for floral lift. Stir; inhale the steam—bright, simple, classic.

2. Lime-Mint Shiver

Pink salt, juice of ½ lime, eight ounces room-temp water, three torn mint leaves. Stir and sip before the mint turns dark; flavor is crisp, mojito-clean.

3. Grapefruit-Thyme Trim

Pink salt, juice of ¼ ruby grapefruit, six ounces warm water, two sprigs fresh thyme lightly crushed. Bitter notes tame appetite for hours.

4. Blood-Orange Glow

Salt, juice of ½ blood orange, eight ounces warm water, micro-grating of fresh ginger. Citrusy spice warms the throat and sparks circulation.

5. Blackberry-Sage Serenade

Salt, one frozen blackberry, juice of ½ lemon, eight ounces water, sage leaf torn once. Berry chills, sage earthiness grounds; sweetness stays gentle.

6. Turmeric Sunrise Silk

Salt, ⅛ teaspoon ground turmeric whisked into eight ounces warm water, juice of ½ lemon, pinch black pepper. Anti-inflammatory resonance without lingering grit.

7. Ginger-Lime Zing

Salt, ¼ teaspoon grated ginger, juice of ½ lime, eight ounces warm water. Immediate nasal wake-up; digestion smiles.

8. Cinnamon-Citrus Comfort

Salt, ⅛ teaspoon Ceylon cinnamon, juice of ½ orange, eight ounces warm water. Tastes like sunrise toast without the carbs.

9. Raspberry-Basil Spark

Salt, one frozen raspberry, juice of ½ lemon, eight ounces water, basil leaf shredded. Color turns pink, flavor dances.

10. Pineapple-Mint Island
Salt, one tablespoon unsweetened pineapple juice, eight ounces water, three mint leaves. Tropical note lifts mood, bromelain eases bloat.

11. Cucumber-Lemon Cool
Salt, four thin cucumber rounds squeezed slightly, juice of ½ lemon, eight ounces chilled water. Spa vibe in sixty seconds.

12. Watermelon-Rosemary Refresher
Salt, tablespoon watermelon juice (mash cube with spoon), eight ounces water, rosemary sprig swirl. Subtle sweetness meets piney aromatics.

13. Honey-Grapefruit Glide
Salt, juice of ½ grapefruit, eight ounces warm water, ½ teaspoon raw honey. Balances bitterness; good for first-time grapefruit skeptics.

14. Matcha-Citrus Lift
Salt, ¼ teaspoon high-quality matcha whisked into two ounces warm water, juice of ½ lemon, six ounces cool water. Gentle green caffeine under mineral guard.

15. Blueberry-Lavender Mist
Salt, five crushed blueberries, juice of ½ lemon, eight ounces water, pinch edible lavender buds. Aroma relaxes; anthocyanins nourish.

16. Apple-Cider Brisk
Salt, one teaspoon raw apple-cider vinegar, eight ounces warm water, dash cinnamon. Metabolic kick without full-force ACV burn.

17. Cherry-Almond Dawn

Salt, three halved cherries (fresh or thawed), eight ounces water, almond extract toothpick-swirl. Black-Forest hint without sugar surge.

18. Strawberry-Balsamic Burst

Salt, one mashed strawberry, eight ounces water, six drops aged balsamic. Gourmet twist, adds polyphenols and complexity.

19. Fig-Vanilla Velvet

Salt, teaspoon fig purée, eight ounces warm water, drop pure vanilla. Creamy illusion without dairy; potassium boost.

20. Cocoa-Orange Ember

Salt, ½ teaspoon raw cacao powder, juice of ½ orange, eight ounces warm water. Morning feels like dessert but fuels mitochondria.

21. Pear-Cardamom Cloud

Salt, tablespoon ripe pear pulp, eight ounces water, pinch ground cardamom. Gentle, fragrant, cough-soothing on brisk days.

Making Variety Effortless

- **Sunday batch prep.** Pre-slice citrus, wash herbs, bag spice blends. Twenty minutes once a week equals dizzying choice on autopilot.
- **Color rule.** Rotate hue daily—yellow, green, pink, orange, purple—to subconsciously confirm nutrient diversity.
- **Temperature toggle.** Warm in winter, cool in summer; your vagus nerve reads warmth as calm, cold as alertness.

Use season and schedule as your guide.

- **Sweet restraint.** If you add honey, maple, or fruit juice, tally no more than two sweetened tonics per week; keep palate sensitive to subtle flavors.

Troubleshooting Flavor Fatigue

If the mineral edge still feels sharp after Day 7:

1. Decrease salt to one-eighth teaspoon for three days, then return to the standard dose.
2. Add a splash of coconut water (rich in potassium) to round corners.
3. Finish with a single ice cube; chilling dulls salinity without diluting minerals significantly.

Within a fortnight your tongue recalibrates, and what once tasted briny becomes the new bright.

Habit Anchors That Stick

- **Pair with sunlight.** Stand near a window; let photons and minerals signal your circadian clock in tandem.
- **Link to breath.** Inhale for four counts while the salt dissolves, exhale for six; nervous system down-shifts before caffeine ever arrives.

- **Share the ritual.** Housemate, partner, or teenager joins? Compliance doubles when witnessed.

Twenty-one options, ninety seconds apiece, zero guesswork. Tomorrow choose one that matches your mood, stir without hurry, and remember: the simplest acts done consistently eclipse complicated regimens abandoned by February. In Chapter 4 we move from the glass to the plate, pairing five-ingredient meals that harmonize with your morning mineral chorus and keep energy steady until nightfall.

Salmon: The Pink-Fleshed Multitasker

A single four-ounce fillet offers:

- **Sodium–potassium balance** forged in ocean currents.
- **Magnesium** tucked beside omega-3s to calm arterial walls.
- **Selenium** (antioxidant bodyguard) and **iodine** for thyroid rhythm.

Five-Ingredient Brine-Baked Salmon (serves 2)

1. Two four-ounce wild salmon fillets
2. One teaspoon pink salt
3. Zest of one lemon
4. Tablespoon fresh dill, chopped
5. Teaspoon olive oil

Lightly coat fillets in oil. Sprinkle salt and lemon zest, press dill onto flesh, bake at 400 °F (205 °C) for 12 minutes. The briny crust seals juices; dill lifts flavor without masking minerals. Plate with a squeeze of lemon—the acid nudges iron absorption upward.

Hemp Tofu: Mineral Gold for Plant-Forward Eaters

Forget soy squabbles; hemp tofu is nutty, light, and naturally boasts magnesium plus plenty of potassium. Its subtle flavor absorbs marinades in ten minutes flat.

Five-Ingredient Crispy Hemp Bites (serves 2)

1. Eight ounces hemp tofu, cubed
2. Tablespoon tamari (gluten-free soy alternative)
3. Half-teaspoon pink salt
4. Teaspoon sesame oil
5. Pinch smoked paprika

Toss cubes with remaining ingredients; air-fry at 375 °F (190 °C) for 8 minutes or roast in a hot skillet. The outside crackles; the inside stays creamy. Serve over wilted greens for a protein-mineral duet.

Roots & Shoots That Spare Insulin

Carbohydrates aren't villains; they're storytellers. The chapter you choose shapes insulin's arc. Low-glycemic roots and shoots whisper rather than shout, keeping post-meal glucose climbs gradual, cortisol calm, and fat storage switches unflipped.

Sweet Potato Medallions

Slice into half-inch rounds, toss with avocado oil, dust with sea salt and rosemary, roast 20 minutes at 425 °F (220 °C). Fiber slows sugar entry; orange flesh contributes beta-carotene for cellular antioxidant defense.

Beet-Top Stir-Down

Beet greens outshine the roots in magnesium and calcium. Sauté briefly with garlic, splash apple-cider vinegar, finish with flaky salt. Two cups raw reduce to one comforting half-cup of silky leaves—earth's own electrolyte gel.

The Color Rule: Build a Dawn-to-Dusk Rainbow

Children who refuse vegetables often respond to a game of colors. Adults do, too. The guideline is simple: **eat at least four distinct hues before nightfall**—not counting the lemon slice in your tonic. Each pigment family houses unique phytonutrients that anchor minerals where they belong.

Color	Micronutrient Stars	Quick Five-Ingredient Example
Red/Pink	Lycopene, betacyanin	Cherry tomato-watermelon salad (tomatoes, watermelon cubes, feta, mint, drizzle balsamic)
Orange/Yellow	Beta-carotene, lutein	Turmeric-roasted carrots (carrots, turmeric, salt, ghee, squeeze of orange)
Green	Chlorophyll, sulforaphane	Flash-steam broccolini (broccolini, garlic, salt, olive oil, lemon zest)
Purple/Blue	Anthocyanins, resveratrol	Blueberry-cabbage slaw (shredded red cabbage, blueberries, salt, yogurt, splash lime)

Why four? Research shows plate diversity correlates with gut-microbe diversity; the more strains you foster, the more short-chain fatty acids you produce—metabolites that reduce visceral fat and keep intestinal walls tight against inflammatory leakage. A color goal simplifies nutrition math into a painter's joy.

One-Pan Sheet-Tray Dinners: Minimal Cleanup, Maximal Electrolytes

The sheet-tray dinner is the home cook's secret handshake—load, roast, walk away. The trick is **ingredient zoning**: pair vegetables that share roast times so nothing burns.

Mediterranean Mineral Mix (serves 4)

Ingredients

1. One pound salmon or hemp tofu cubes
2. Two cups cherry tomatoes
3. One cup sliced zucchini
4. One cup bell-pepper strips
5. Half a cup pitted olives

Method

1. Pre-heat oven to 425 °F (220 °C).
2. Brush tray with olive oil, lay salmon center, surround with veg, scatter olives.
3. Sprinkle one teaspoon pink salt, cracked pepper, oregano.
4. Roast 15–17 minutes until salmon flakes and tomatoes blister.

Tomatoes burst, releasing juice that mingles with salmon drippings to create an unofficial sauce infused with sodium and potassium. Serve over baby spinach; residual heat wilts greens for free.

Sunday Batch Hacks for Readers Who "Hate Cooking"

1. **Quarter Hour Chop-Storm**
   Set a timer for 15 minutes. Dice onions, bell peppers, zucchini, carrots; portion into mason jars. When hunger ambushes mid-week, vegetables are step-zero ready.

2. **Double Protein, Half Effort**
   Roast two trays of salmon or hemp tofu at once. Refrigerate half. Cold leftovers flake into lunchtime salads or breakfast omelets without complaint.

3. **Mineral Broth Cubes**
   Simmer pink salt, kombu seaweed, celery tops, and carrot peels for one hour. Freeze in silicone cubes. Drop a cube into boiling water to transform plain quinoa or rice into mineral-rich sides.

4. **Color Bag**
   Keep a gallon zip bag in the freezer labeled "Rainbow." Each time you prep produce, toss in leftover broccoli stems, beet tops, or herb ends. By week's end, you own a free stir-fry blend.

5. **Zero-Waste Citrus Zest Dust**

Zest all lemons and limes before juicing for tonics. Spread zest thin on parchment, air-dry overnight. Store in a jar; pinch over sheet-tray dinners for aroma that costs nothing and boosts vitamin C.

A Day on the Plate — Sample Blueprint

Time	Meal	Ingredients	Mineral & Hormone Rationale
6:30 a.m.	*Pink-Salt Tonic*	Lemon-Rose Dawn	Sodium-potassium hydration, magnesium spark
8:00 a.m.	*Breakfast*	Two soft-boiled eggs over beet-top stir-down, slice sweet-potato medallions	Protein + magnesium rich greens + slow-carb root
12:30 p.m.	*Lunch*	Leftover salmon flakes, mixed greens, blueberry-lavender vinaigrette	Omega-3s calm cortisol dip; anthocyanins boost insulin sensitivity
3:30 p.m.	*Snack*	Hemp tofu crispy bite, cucumber rounds	Stabilizes blood sugar, adds potassium without sugar spike
6:30 p.m.	*Dinner*	Mediterranean Mineral Mix; squeeze charred lemon	One-pan ease, full color rule, selenium, iodine support
8:45 p.m.	*Evening Wind-Down*	Herbal tea with pinch cream of tartar	Potassium relieves nighttime muscle twitch; balances sodium day load

No macros to tally, no apps to curse. You ate four distinct colors, balanced electrolytes, spared insulin sharp peaks—mission met.

When Cravings Crash the Party

If an evening sweet tooth sneaks past mineral guardians, blend one frozen banana disk with a teaspoon raw cacao, pinch pink salt, splash almond milk—whipped in 30 seconds to sorbet. The salt accentuates chocolate depth; magnesium signals "all clear" to the hypothalamus. Craving thanks you and sits down quietly.

Micronutrients, Macro Wins

You won't find calorie counts here. Instead, trust the rule that **food richest in minerals satiates first.** Studies reveal diets high in sodium-potassium balance and magnesium density lead to lower total caloric intake, not through restriction but through early satiety signals reaching the brain in real time. Five ingredients per dish compel you to choose potent, unprocessed components—nothing left over for fillers or hidden sugars.

The Unseen Commitments

Real-food amplifiers aren't about culinary perfection; they're about honoring tiny agreements:

1. **I will keep salt unbleached and intentional.**
2. **I will invite color onto every plate.**
3. **I will let the oven rescue my schedule.**
4. **I will treat Sunday as a gift to Wednesday Self.**

Hold these promises, and your cells will reciprocate in mitochondrial currency: ATP, clarity, warmth behind the sternum that feels suspiciously like confidence.

Transitioning Forward

You now wield a mineral-rich dawn and plates that hum the same frequency. In Chapter 5 we'll add movement micro-bursts—three-minute stretches and breath ladders that act like bellows on the metabolic fire you've kindled. No gym bag needed. Until then, open your pantry, count ingredients on one hand, and let dinner's aroma remind you that simplicity isn't lack; it's mastery.

Chapter 5

Micro-Bursts

Three-Minute Moves That Turbo-Charge Lymph Flow

There's a secret hallway between the tonic you sip at dawn and the plate you fill at dusk. It isn't paved with miles of cardio, nor lined in chrome-and-neon gym machines. It's a series of narrow doorways—three minutes wide—through which blood, lymph, and confidence can slip any time the day tries to stiffen you into a chair-shaped statue. Step through often enough and metabolism stops feeling like a smoldering ember and starts behaving like a playful flame.

The Power of Three Minutes

Why three? Because it's shorter than a coffee-maker cycle, too brief for the self-sabotaging phrase *"I'll do it later,"* and long enough to flush stagnant lymph, wake sleepy fascia, and coax parasympathetic calm. These micro-bursts are the kinetic cousin of your sixty-second mineral ritual: minimal friction, maximum return.

Fascia-Wake at the Kitchen Counter

Fascia—the gossamer web encasing muscles and organs—loves glide. When dawn finds it dehydrated, it clings to itself like plastic wrap, limiting range and trapping inflammatory metabolites. One tonic won't loosen fascia alone; movement must follow fluid.

Counter Curl & Sweep (90 seconds)

1. Plant palms shoulder-width on the countertop edge, feet hip-width, knees soft.
2. Exhale, tuck tailbone slightly, and roll upper back until shoulder blades spread. Feel a stretch from knuckle to hip.
3. Inhale, ripple chest forward, tilt pelvis back, creating the opposite curve.
4. Repeat for ten breaths—moving as slowly as honey drips—until spine feels warm and wrists awake.

Diagonal Reach & Reset (60 seconds)

1. Stand side-on to the counter, inside hand resting lightly.
2. Outer arm sweeps overhead on an inhale, ribs expanding toward the ceiling.
3. Exhale, bend knees, fold torso diagonally across the body, sliding free hand toward opposite ankle.
4. Three slow reps per side coax fluid through oblique slings—the fascial highways that rotate trunk and propel walking efficiency.

Toe-Tip Calf Melt (30 seconds)
Face counter again, lift onto tiptoes, then drop heels quickly but without thud. Ten pulses create a micro-vacuum in calf veins, sucking blood back to the heart, priming muscles for the day's steps.

Total time: three minutes. Result: a buzz behind the kneecaps, warmth along spine, mind clear enough to taste lemon in your next sip.

Salt & Sweat: Debunking the Mineral-Loss Myth

Your new ritual delivers sodium, potassium, and magnesium in a calibrated sip. Some readers worry short bursts of movement will "sweat out" those gains. Reality: a three-minute fascia flow or calf pump releases far less sodium than a 30-minute run, and the minerals lost come largely from the film of interstitial fluid sitting just under skin—easily replaced by your tonic and regular hydration.

Sweat's real magic is in moving lymph—a slow, valveless river that relies on muscle contractions to ferry metabolic waste. Think of sodium as the ticket you hand sweat glands so they'll flush debris; the price is trivial compared with the cleansing service rendered. Keep sipping, keep moving, and let the loop self-correct.

Desk-Break Calf Pumps for Venous Return

Long Zoom calls shrink ankles behind computer screens. Blood pools, CO_2 lingers, brain fog creeps. Enter the ninety-second desk-break:

1. **Scoot forward** on your chair, feet flat.
2. **Press toes** into the floor, lifting heels high; squeeze calves hard for a two-count.
3. **Drop heels**, lift toes, feeling stretch in shin.
4. Alternate for sixty seconds—pumping blood north.
5. **Finish** with ten rapid ankle circles each direction to swirl lymph trapped near malleoli.

Bonus: the rhythmic squeeze-release cadence tells the vagus nerve the body is in motion, lowering stress chemistry without leaving the meeting.

Breath Ladders: 4-7-8 Meets Box Breathing

Oxygen is a nutrient, carbon dioxide a messenger, and controlled breath a gearshift straight into parasympathetic serenity. Combine two proven patterns into a ladder that fits inside three minutes.

1. **Exhale fully** through mouth for a count of **8**.
2. Inhale gently through nose for **4**.

3. Hold at the top for **4**—feeling ribcage broaden.

4. Exhale again for **8**—long, slow, shoulder-dropping.

5. Hold empty for **4**.

That completes one rung. Climb three rungs and notice fingertips tingle as CO_2 levels balance cerebral blood flow. Your next task will feel easier, not because it shrank but because mental grip strengthened.

Pair breath ladders with calf pumps and your seated minutes transform from metabolic stall to subtle engine idle—ready to rev.

The Stick-Up Mobility Calendar

Consistency outperforms intensity. Print a single-page calendar and tape it where eyes land daily—the fridge, monitor bezel, or bathroom mirror. Mark each day with four simple icons:

- **Sunrise Stretch** (kitchen-counter fascia wake)
- **Desk Pump** (calf circuit)
- **Breath Ladder** (three-rung cycle)
- **Evening Stroll** (ten-minute walk after dinner)

Aim to mark at least **three icons** every day. Miss a morning? Make up with an extra breath ladder before lunch. The visual streak sparks dopamine reinforcement, turning micro-bursts into second nature.

After one month, discard the paper—habits now live in muscle memory and brainstem, not on walls.

When and How to Layer Micro-Bursts

- **Immediately after your tonic** – counter stretches hydrate fascia just awakened by minerals.
- **Mid-morning lull (10–11 a.m.)** – calf pumps and breath ladder prevent snack-seeking driven by blood-flow dip.
- **Pre-lunch reboot** – a thirty-second diagonal reach and reset sharpens appetite signals, helping you stop at satisfied rather than stuffed.
- **Late-afternoon slump** – repeat the full three-minute routine to sweep away cytokines accumulated from desktop posture.
- **Post-dinner stroll** – digestion speeds, glucose peaks lower, sleep hormones cue earlier.

Five mini-sessions total fewer minutes than one sitcom episode but scatter metabolic glitter across the day.

Ritual, Not Regiment

You don't need spandex or sneakers. Most of these moves are performed barefoot or in office flats. Their genius is stealth:

co-workers assume you're stretching; family thinks you're merely contemplative at the counter. Meanwhile, lymph channels unclog, cortisol clocks rewind, and the mineral message broadcast at dawn echoes louder in every cell.

Let three minutes be your rebel yawn against sedentary culture. Tomorrow morning when wristwatch hits that sixty-second tonic mark, slide palms onto the countertop and begin the dance. The flame you lit with salt deserves a bellows. Breathe, stretch, pump, and feel the ember swell.

Chapter 6

Mind Over Morning

Taming Cravings at the Neurological Source

Morning begins with minerals, but it ends—too often—with a stealth attack from the pantry: a pastry you didn't plan, a second latte melting discipline into foam. This chapter dissects that ambush at its command center—your brain's reward circuitry—and arms you with tools to rewrite the script before cravings ever clear their throats.

The Biochemistry of Wanting

Cravings are not flaws in character; they are electrical codes. The chief scribe is dopamine, a neurotransmitter evolved to tag survival behaviours as pleasurable. In ancestral life it pulsed when we found ripe fruit after scarcity. In modern life it spikes when the delivery app dings.

Here's the catch: dopamine fires on **anticipation**, not consumption. Once you bite, levels taper and cortisol creeps back, urging another bite to recapture the thrill. This loop repeats until the stomach rebels or guilt interrupts.

Minerals, meanwhile, govern neuronal voltage. Adequate sodium and potassium keep action potentials precise; magnesium reins in glutamate's excitatory chatter. When dawn delivers electrolytes, neurons signal "resources secured," reducing the baseline angst that primes dopamine for cheap wins. A calm nervous system wants nourishment, not novelty.

Two-Minute Dawn Visualization

While your tonic steeps and cools, borrow one-hundred-and-twenty seconds to reroute neurochemistry. Stand or sit where sunrise reaches skin. Eyes soft, jaw unclenched.

1. **Frame the future.** Picture yourself three hours ahead, working or parenting, yet feeling a gentle hum behind the sternum—energy without tension. Notice colours, sounds, pace of breath.

2. **Zoom to the fork.** See the moment cravings usually strike: vending machine, bakery display, restless fridge door. Freeze-frame it.

3. **Insert mineral memory.** In that still image, imagine a warm tide moving from collarbone to pelvis—your dawn tonic diffusing cell by cell. Feel its steadiness overriding the sugar siren.

4. **Anchor a gesture.** Press thumb to middle finger—light, deliberate. This touch will become your portable switch; any time cravings surface, mimic the gesture to cue the full-body memory of calm.

5. **Release and step forward.** Exhale through the nose; open eyes. Drink the tonic, tasting the future you just rehearsed.

Neuroscientists call this mental time travel "episodic future thinking." It props open the gap between impulse and action long enough for the prefrontal cortex to decide, not the midbrain.

Journal Question: "What Is Hungry Inside Me?"

Keep a slim notebook beside the salt jar. Each morning, before first sip, write today's date and the prompt:

> What is hungry inside me?

Let the answer sprawl for sixty seconds—grammar indifferent, honesty high. Patterns emerge:

- **Fatigue hunger** (I slept six broken hours)
- **Emotional hunger** (Yesterday's argument still echoes)
- **Boredom hunger** (Digital monotony at work)
- **Nutrient hunger** (Muscles ache for protein after workout)

Naming dissolves amorphous desire into solvable categories. By week's end you can match remedies: nap, phone-free walk, laughter call, salmon salad. The page becomes a map of authentic needs that processed sugar can never satisfy.

Sleep Architecture and Pink-Salt Dreams

Night either re-stitches neural fabric or unravels it. Short, fractured sleep raises ghrelin—the hunger hormone—by sunrise while throttling leptin—the satiety signal. Enter glycine, an amino acid abundant in collagen and, in small measure, pink salt's trace mineral matrix.

Glycine slips through the blood-brain barrier and cues the ventrolateral preoptic nucleus to drop core temperature, deepening slow-wave sleep. When you combine glycine-rich mineral intake with a pre-bed ritual—herbal tea plus a pinch of cream of tartar for potassium—sleep stages lengthen and cortisol's morning peak lowers. Lower peak, fewer cravings.

Build a **Pink-Salt Dream Stack**:

- **Dinner** – protein with connective tissue: salmon skin crisped, chicken drumsticks, or bone-broth quinoa.
- **Evening tonic** – 8 oz warm water, pinch cream of tartar, squeeze of lemon.
- **Wind-down cue** – same thumb-to-finger gesture from morning visualization, anchoring body memory of calm at both bookends of the day.

Within a week, REM-to-wake transitions feel like sliding silk, not jerking gravel. Cravings lose their foothold when rest is whole.

Putting It All Together — A Dawn-to-Dusk Neural Loop

1. **60-Second Mineral Switch** (physiology)
2. **2-Minute Visualization** (cognition)
3. **1-Minute Journal Answer** (emotion)
4. **Three-Minute Micro-Burst Stretch** (circulation)
5. **Colour-Rich Meals** (satiety)
6. **Evening Dream Stack** (recovery)

Total added time: roughly ten minutes. Outcomes: steady glucose curve, trimmed snack frequency, clear head, lighter waist.

Tomorrow's Invitation

Set notebook and pen beside the jar tonight. At dawn, before the world edits your agenda, ask the question, write the truth, see the future, sip the minerals. Thumb meets finger—click, the new loop engages.

Cravings are conversations. Teach them a new language, and they stop shouting; they start negotiating. That negotiation leaves space—space to create, to play, to rest without guilt. In Chapter 7, we'll channel that freed bandwidth into the 14-Day Quick-Start, translating everything you've learned into a living, trackable rhythm.

Until then, sleep deeply, wake curious, and remember: the hungriest part of you is often thirsting for minerals and meaning, not sugar.

Part 3

SUSTAIN

KnowHowLeaf Publishing

Chapter 7

The 14-Day Quick-Start

Fourteen dawns. That is all this chapter asks of you. Two short weeks to knit the mineral switch, color-rich plates, micro-bursts, and mindset cues into a lived rhythm—long enough for the brain to file them under *automatic*, short enough that motivation stays lively. Think of these pages as a flight manual: you will taxi, lift, level out, and land, all while tracking the gauges that matter most.

The Daily Playbook

1 · **Mineral Minute (wake + 60 s)**

- Quarter-teaspoon pink salt, citrus of choice.
- While it cools: two-minute future-visualization, thumb-to-finger anchor.

2 · **Fascia Wake-Up (wake + 3 min)**

- Counter Curl & Sweep → Diagonal Reach → Toe-Tip Calf Melt.

3 · Breakfast Window (within 90 min of waking)

- Protein centric (eggs, hemp tofu) + one low-glycemic root or shoot.
- Add one color you did **not** drink in the tonic—keep the rainbow score climbing.

4 · Mid-Morning Micro-Burst (10–11 a.m.)

- Desk-break calf pumps + breath ladder (three rungs).
- Eight-ounce water rinse; add a pinch of salt only if sweat or caffeine intake felt high.

5 · Lunch Lens

- Plate must show at least **three colors**; include healthy fat (avocado, olive oil) to escort fat-soluble minerals into cells.

6 · Afternoon Reset (3 p.m.)

- If cravings whisper, gesture anchor first.
- Drink 12 oz water; add potassium-rich cream of tartar pinch if legs feel heavy.
- Option: 60-second tonic half-dose for long workdays or hot climates.

7 · Evening Plate & Stroll

- Sheet-tray dinner or leftover batch meal.
- Ten-minute walk → lymph flush + glucose flatten.

8 · Dream Stack (1 h before bed)

- Herbal tea, pinch potassium, glycine-rich snack (bone-broth sip or collagen square).
- One breath ladder rung to dim nervous system.

Repeat. Simplicity is the superpower.

The Fast-Feedback Worksheet

Tear a fresh sheet of paper, rule four vertical columns, label:

1. **Energy** (1–10) — mid-morning spark.
2. **Bloating** (F, P, N) — flat, puffy, normal.
3. **Cravings** (0–3) — none, gentle, strong.
4. **Mood** — sunny to overcast.

Each night, log the day in thirty seconds. Patterns appear fast:

- Energy up, cravings down by Day 4? Sodium-potassium dial is right.
- Bloating persists? Increase leafy greens, reduce raw crucifers at dinner.
- Mood cloudy after poor sleep? Double glycine snack; guard bedtime screen.

By Day 14 the sheet reads like a weather map turning from turbulent gray to stable gold.

Week-One Focus: Hydration & Hue

- **Goal:** Hit mineral switch plus **two** distinct plate colors daily.
- **Watch for:** Early salt adaptation—mild thirst or loose stool; remedy with extra potassium foods (spinach, coconut water).
- **Celebrate:** First 0.5-inch loss at waist or first afternoon you forget coffee exists.

Week-Two Focus: Rhythm & Refinement

- **Goal:** Fold in **all four** micro-burst at least five days.
- **Watch for:** Evening sodium creep (chips, cured meats) masking real progress. Swap with roasted pumpkin seeds dusted in smoked paprika.
- **Celebrate:** Energy scale averages two points higher than your Day-1 baseline; cravings column peppered with zeros.

The Forgiveness Clause

Perfectionism is a saboteur dressed as discipline. If you miss a tonic, oversleep, or dive mouth-first into a brownie, circle the day's row on your worksheet. That circle is a campfire, not a scar. Write one sentence: *"Data, not drama."* Tomorrow, resume exactly where the playbook left off—no doubling salt, no fasting penance. The body thrives on consistency, not punishment.

Common Detours & Mid-Air Corrections

- **Day 3 headache?** Likely caffeine withdrawal or glycogen shift. Add magnesium (pumpkin seeds) and half-dose tonic mid-afternoon.
- **Salt tastes too intense?** Dilute with two extra ounces water; taste buds recalibrate within a week.
- **Scale static but measurements down?** Intracellular water rising; celebrate.
- **Travel day disrupts routine?** Carry single-serve salt packets and herb tea bags; walk airport corridors for calf pumps.

Landing the Fortnight

On night fourteen, tally worksheet trends. Circle highest Energy score, lowest Cravings score. Compare waistline or the looseness of favorite jeans. If progress sings, glide straight into the optional 28-Day Challenge in Chapter 8. If numbers lag, audit:

- **Salt dose:** Adjust up or down by ⅛ tsp.

- **Color count:** Did plates hit four hues?
- **Sleep quality:** Dream Stack followed at least five nights?
- **Micro-burst compliance:** Three icons average?

Tune, recommit, and repeat another seven days before judging. Metabolism is a choir; allow time for harmony.

Fourteen dawns. That's the deal. Keep the agreement and you'll step into the next chapter lighter, clearer, and armed with proof—not hope—that your body responds to mineral rhythm and compassionate consistency. Chapter 8 will stretch the horizon to twenty-eight days, layering community and printable tools so the habit outlives momentum. For tonight, pin your worksheet where morning eyes will meet it. Tomorrow, the pen records evidence of change.

Chapter 8

The 28-Day Pink Salt Challenge & Printable Success Journal

Fourteen dawns proved that minerals, color-rich food, micro-bursts, and mindset cues can braid into a livable rhythm.

Now we zoom out to a full lunar cycle—**28 days**—long enough to re-pattern hormones, remodel connective tissue, and let the brain rewire habit loops into default settings.

Consider this chapter your expedition map: four themed base-camps, daily checkpoints, a communal campsite, and a journal that turns progress into ink.

How the Challenge Works

Element	Why it matters	How you'll use it
Weekly Focus Theme	Gives each 7-day block a single victory target, so energy stays sharp and measurable.	Study the overview on Day 0; print it; post it.
Habit-Stack Triad	Anchors the day at sunrise, noon, and sunset—three neural "bookmarks" the brain remembers.	Follow the triad matrix (p 11) until autopilot emerges.
Success Journal	Converts feelings into data, data into motivation.	Fill the PDF each night—never skip more than 48 hours.
Community Hub	Social proof and micro-competitions fire dopamine in service of your goals.	Scan the QR, choose a username, log points.
Forgiveness Clause	Keeps the perfectionist offstage.	Miss a task? Circle the date, write "Data—Not Drama," continue.

WEEK 1 · ELECTROLYTE AWAKENING

Objective: Saturate cells with balanced minerals, calibrate tonic dose, master two daily colors.

Sunrise Window	Noon Reset	Sunset Close-Out
· Standard tonic	· 12 oz water + ⅛ tsp salt	· Sheet-tray dinner
· 2-min visualization	· Breath ladder x 2	· 10-min stroll
· Counter fascia flow	· Color check: add missing hue at lunch	· Journal lines 1–3

Pro-Tips

- **Dose-Check:** If ankles swell by Day 3, drop salt to ⅛ tsp; if afternoon fog lingers, bump to ⅓ tsp.
- **Color Shortcut:** Frozen berry medley counts as purple/blue; toss into Greek yogurt or hemp parfait.

- **Cathedral Posture:** Each time you walk through a doorway, roll shoulders back—free posture reset.

WEEK 2 · HORMONE HARMONY

Objective: Smooth cortisol peaks, nurture thyroid, and align mineral rhythm with menstrual or circadian cycle.

Sunrise Window	Noon Reset	Sunset Close-Out
· Add adaptogen option (maca in tonic #11 or as capsule) · 3-min gratitude breath	· Potassium plus protein (avocado-chicken wrap) · Desk-pump calves	· Glycine Dream Stack · 5-min restorative stretch · Journal lines 1–5

Cycle-Specific Adjustments

- **Luteal Week (PMS):** Double magnesium foods—pumpkin seeds, dark chocolate, leafy greens.
- **Follicular Week:** Extend micro-burst to 5 min; strength gains peak.

WEEK 3 · METABOLIC MOMENTUM

Objective: Raise NEAT (non-exercise activity thermogenesis); train mitochondria with gentle intensity bumps.

Sunrise Window	Noon Reset	Sunset Close-Out
· Standard tonic + matcha twist #14 on alternate days	· 4-min brisk stair climb + breath ladder	· 15-min walk or 7-min bodyweight circuit · Protein-heavy plate

Momentum Moves

1. **Pomodoro Pace:** Every 25 min of desk work = 60 sec standing sway or calf pump.
2. **Color-Plus Rule:** Add fermented accent (kimchi, sauerkraut) to one meal—microbiome turbo.
3. **Social Sprint:** Post a tonic photo to hub; earn "Spark" badge (25 pts).

WEEK 4 · FAT-BURN FINALE

Objective: Enhance fat oxidation, lock habits into identity, plot long-term maintenance.

Sunrise Window	Noon Reset	Sunset Close-Out
· Optional half-dose tonic + 12-hour fast (last meal 8 p.m.)	· Protein + high-fiber root (sweet-potato medallions)	· Dream Stack + 4-7-8 breath ladder · Write tomorrow's menu

Finisher Challenges

- **Rainbow Relay:** Hit five colors in one day (50 pts).
- **Silent Sunrise:** Digital-free first hour (30 pts).
- **Vault Walk:** Accumulate 70 k steps this week (badge + brag rights).

HABIT-STACK MATRIX (Print & Pin)

Time	Trigger	Action	Why it works
Sunrise	Alarm off → Kitchen	Tonic + visualization	Pairing movement with existing cue = near-zero friction
Noon	Lunch plate hits table	Water + breath ladder	Appetite regulation & vagus-nerve reset
Sunset	Dinner dishes done	10-min walk	Lowers post-prandial glucose, primes melatonin

SUCCESS JOURNAL TEMPLATE

Pink Salt ◦ 28-Day Success Journal Day ___ / 28

(Complete each field in under 2 minutes. Four+ colors & all icons = gold star day.)

1 Mineral Minute

Time tonic ⏰_____ Salt ___ tsp

Exact clock time + dose sharpen your personal formula.

2 Color Radar (circle)

4+ hues feed gut diversity & hormones

3 Micro-Burst Icons (circle as you go)

Sunrise stretch   Noon desk-pump   Breath ladder   Evening stroll

4 Cravings & Energy

Time	10 am	3 pm	9 pm
Cravings 0-3	__	__	__
Energy 1-10	__	__	__

5 Bloat / Mood (circle)

Bloat F P N   Mood

6 Metrics (optional, weekly)

Waist ___ in Hips ___ in Weight ___ lb

7 Gratitude Flash

One sentence to close the day: ____

1

Page Layout (one day per page)

Section	How to fill	Purpose
1. Mineral Minute	Time consumed / dose	Correlate timing with energy
2. Color Count	Mark hues eaten ( )	Ensures phytonutrient spread
3. Micro-Burst Icons	(circle completed)	Quick compliance snapshot
4. Cravings Graph	Plot 0–3 scale at 10 a.m., 3 p.m., 9 p.m.	Visual trigger vs mineral link
5. Bloat & Mood Log	F / P / N & emoji	Pattern spotter
6. Measurement Stripe	Waist, hip, weight (optional)	Trend over 28 days
7. Gratitude Square	One sentence: "Today I'm grateful for..."	Neuroplasticity toward positivity

Print or annotate digitally; total nightly fill-time: 3–4 min.

SAMPLE DAY WALK-THROUGH

Task	Done?	Insight
Tonic at 6:42 a.m.	✓	Dose stable at ¼ tsp
Colors (red, green, orange)	✓	Need purple/blue tomorrow
Micro-Bursts		Missed evening walk—rain
Cravings graph	0-1-1	Evening sweet urge ↓ after tea
Bloat/Mood	N /	Progress!
Gratitude	"Laughing with my daughter over burnt toast"	Warm finish

WHAT SUCCESS LOOKS LIKE

- Waistline softer or jeans button easier.
- Energy graph averaging at least two points higher.
- Cravings curve flat or predictable.

- Sleep cycles deeper; dream recall better.
- Mineral ritual and micro-bursts feel odd **to skip**—identity shift achieved.

After Day 28

1. **Choose a Path**
    - **Maintain:** Keep triad; ease off badges.
    - **Evolve:** Start gentle intermittent-fasting window; retain morning mineral.
    - **Expand:** Follow to Book B's deep recipe library.
2. **Celebrate Intentionally**
   Host a pink-salt brunch, share rainbow plates, post final badge totals.
3. **Archive the Journal**
   Flip through pages; note theme of growth > loss. Store as baseline for next venture.

Dawn is now a well-worn doorway, not an experiment. Step through tomorrow knowing electrolytes, color, breath, stretch, and community await on the other side—no willpower required, only invitation. The Fat-Burn Finale isn't an ending; it is a launchpad toward whatever chapter of vitality calls next.

Part 4

THRIVE

KnowHowLeaf Publishing

Chapter 9

Plateaus, Travel Days, and Curveballs

You have crossed twenty-eight dawns, the mineral switch is instinct, and your body hums with a steadier rhythm. Yet life is neither laboratory nor monastery; it throws detours—long flights, client dinners, menstrual cycles that hijack cravings, an unexpected flu that steals appetite. This chapter equips you to meet those curveballs with the same calm confidence you now feel at sunrise. Think of it as the living appendix to everything you have built: practical, portable, and forgiving.

When the Tonic Tastes "Wrong" Abroad

Change your latitude, change your water—and sometimes your trusted pink-salt tonic morphs from bright to briny or, worse, vaguely metallic. The culprit is usually the mineral profile of local municipal water.

- **Hard water** (rich in calcium and magnesium) can flatten citrus tang and over-accentuate saltiness.
- **Soft water** (low mineral content, often sodium-treated) can make the tonic taste thin or oddly sweet.

Rapid recalibration

1. **Taste test first.** Sip two ounces of plain tap water to gauge baseline.

2. **Adjust salt, not citrus.** In hard-water regions cut salt dose by one-sixteenth teaspoon and keep lemon constant; in soft-water regions add one-sixteenth teaspoon salt and consider a few drops of magnesium citrate.

3. **Filter on the fly.** A pocket-sized carbon filter bottle reduces chlorine that can clash with mineral notes.

4. **Buy still spring water.** European and many Asian markets stock glass bottles listing bicarbonate, calcium, and sodium levels—choose moderate profiles (sodium < 50 mg/L, calcium < 150 mg/L) for a neutral canvas.

5. **Trust temperature.** Slightly warmer water softens harsh hard-water edges; cooler water perks up flat soft-water tonics.

Within two mornings your palate adjusts; within four you may not notice the difference at all—but your cells will continue to recognise the mineral signal.

Restaurant Ordering Scripts: Electrolytes First

Business lunch, birthday brunch, last-minute airport bistro—menus seldom advertise mineral density. Use these scripts to keep your electrolyte foundation intact without sounding like the high-maintenance diner at the table.

Scenario	Say This	Why It Works
Sit-down dinner	"Could I have sparkling water with a lemon wedge and, if possible, a pinch of sea salt on the side?"	Staff deliver bread with salt; asking for a pinch raises no eyebrows. Sparkling water's bicarbonate balances sodium.
Breakfast café	"I'd love two soft-boiled eggs and avocado slices. Can you sprinkle a little coarse sea salt on top?"	Eggs supply choline; avocado potassium. Coarse salt signals mineral intent without special prep.
Airport fast casual	"Grilled chicken salad, dressing on the side, extra lime wedge please." At the register, grab a packet of sea salt; crumble half over greens.	Most salad bars use iodised salt indoors; your packet re-establishes sodium-potassium ratio.
Italian restaurant	"I'll have the grilled salmon but swap the mashed potatoes for sautéed spinach. And could the kitchen finish with flaky salt and lemon zest?"	Salmon + spinach = sodium, potassium, magnesium. Lemon zest mirrors tonic chemistry.
Shared tapas	"Let's add marinated olives and roasted peppers to the spread."	Olives supply sodium; peppers add vitamin C to aid mineral uptake.

Notes for stealth: Speak with warmth, keep requests concise, praise the server. Hospitality culture rewards kindness with better compliance.

Menstrual-Cycle Tweaks & Perimenopause Pivots

Hormones ride a month-long carousel; minerals are the rails that keep the ride smooth. Fine-tune tonic and meal timing to match each phase.

Phase	Days*	Body Chemistry	Tonic / Food Adjustments
Menstruation	1-5	Iron dips, prostaglandins spike inflammation.	Add ½ tsp blackstrap molasses to morning tonic; iron + minerals soothe cramps. Pair with vitamin C fruit to boost absorption.
Follicular	6-13	Estrogen climbs; insulin sensitivity high.	Keep standard tonic; explore sweeter tonics (pineapple-mint) if cravings mild. Include moderate carbs post-workout.
Ovulation	14-16	LH surge; energy peaks.	Maintain tonic; hydration paramount. Post-workout add electrolyte tablet in water. Focus on lean protein to support tissue repair.
Luteal	17-28	Progesterone rises then falls; sodium pulled intracellularly; cravings intensify.	Double tonic frequency (dawn + mid-afternoon). Increase magnesium foods—pumpkin seeds, dark chocolate. Replace evening walk with slower yin stretch to calm cortisol.

*Lengths vary—track your own calendar.

Perimenopause pivots

Fluctuating estrogen can cause salt-water retention swings. If morning rings feel tight, drop sodium by one-eighth teaspoon for three days while increasing potassium-rich produce; if energy slumps, restore original dose. Hot flashes respond well to chilled tonic variation: add crushed mint, chill overnight, sip at the first heat wave—cooling plus mineral top-up in one gesture.

Restart Protocol After Illness or Vacation

Influenza flattens appetite; beach getaways flatten discipline. Either way, you return home with mineral stores skewed and routines rusty. The temptation: overcorrect with austerity. The solution: gentle triage that respects physiology.

Day 1 — Rehydrate & Re-mineralise

- **Tonic**: full dose upon waking, half-dose at 2 p.m.
- **Food**: bone-broth soup (sodium, glycine) with steamed greens (potassium).
- **Movement**: five-minute breath-ladder walk only; body is still in repair mode.

Day 2 — Reactivate Micro-Bursts

- **Tonic**: standard dawn dose.
- **Food**: five-ingredient plate hitting three colors.

- **Movement:** sunrise fascia wake-up, desk calf pumps, ten-minute sunset stroll.
- **Mindset:** journal "What is hungry inside me?" refresh—illness often muddles cues.

Day 3 — Resume Quick-Start Grid
Return to 14-Day Playbook. If travel weight gain bothers you, note waist not scale; water retention subsides within five days of mineral balance.

When Plateau Fears Tap Your Shoulder

Weight stalls, energy flats, cravings flicker. Before despair, audit:

1. **Salt drift.** Restaurant meals and salted snacks creep upward, throwing sodium-potassium harmony. Test one day at reduced dose; observe morning waist.
2. **Color shrink.** Busy weeks recycle same foods; phytonutrient holes blunt mitochondria. Add a purple or blue plant daily for a week—anthocyanins revive insulin sensitivity.
3. **Sleep debt.** Anything < 7 hours three nights running resets cortisol baseline higher. Reinstate Dream Stack, magnesium, glycine snack.
4. **Micro-burst erosion.** Calendar slipped from four icons to two. Re-print mobility grid; tick boxes publicly on fridge.
5. **Thirst misreads.** Winter air or airplane A/C suppress thirst.

Set phone timer: eight ounces water every two hours; add single salt crystal each second glass.

Plateaus rarely signal failure—usually adaptation. A two-week re-calibration using these audits restores downward trend or upward energy without drastic cuts.

Emergency Kit for Unplanned Chaos

Packets small enough for purse or glovebox:

- **Sea-salt sachets** (⅛ tsp each)
- **Magnesium citrate powder sticks**
- **Collagen single-serve**
- **Freeze-dried berries** (color rescue)
- **Herbal tea bag** (evening wind-down)
- **Tiny journal card & pen** (gratitude square travel size)

When flight delays stretch, conferences overrun, or family emergencies erupt, this kit anchors the mineral-mindset loop wherever you stand.

Thriving Is a Moving Target

Harmony is not stillness; it is dynamic balance—like a surfer adjusting micro-movements to stay on the wave. You now carry the core moves: mineral ignition, color rhythm, micro-bursts, breath ladders, journal reflection, community support. Plateaus, travel, hormones, illness—each is a ripple the ocean throws. Adjust dosage, swap colors, slow or speed movement, and ride on.

In the final chapter we will zoom past the 30-day mark to see how to cycle these practices through seasons, integrate fasting or keto if desired, and keep sunrise precious even as life expands. For now, print the audit list, stock your emergency kit, and greet tomorrow's curveball with a quiet smile.

Chapter 10

Beyond Thirty Days

Future-Proofing Your Mineral Momentum

Thirty sunrises ago you stirred a glass of warm water, pink salt, and lemon, unsure what would happen next. Today that ritual is second nature—an unthinking gesture as familiar as brushing your teeth. This chapter looks farther down the shoreline: six months, a full year, the quiet decades ahead. How do you keep mineral momentum vibrant when seasons shift, tastes evolve, or new health goals beckon? The answer lies in smart cycling, optional paths, and community that grows as you do.

Seasonal Cycling – Salt Tonics in Living Color

Electrolyte needs ebb and flow with temperature, daylight, and produce availability. Rather than forcing one tonic forever, rotate ingredients to match the calendar. Your taste buds stay curious, your micronutrient spectrum widens, and you reinforce the quiet understanding that health is dialogue, not dogma.

Season	Produce Spotlight	Tonic Twist	Mineral Rationale
Spring	Strawberries, mint, young spinach	Strawberry-Mint Spark: muddle a berry, tear two mint leaves, stir into standard tonic	Vitamin C boosts iron uptake; mint stimulates bile flow after winter heaviness
Summer	Watermelon, basil, cucumber	Watermelon-Basil Chill: tablespoon juice + basil leaf, serve over ice	Extra potassium counters heat-driven sodium loss
Autumn	Apple, ginger, beet	Apple-Ginger Warmth: teaspoon raw apple-cider vinegar + coin of ginger	ACV steadies post-harvest carb load; ginger aids lymph when temps drop
Winter	Blood orange, cinnamon, rosemary	Blood-Orange Ember: juice of half blood orange + pinch cinnamon	Citrus polyphenols combat indoor air stress; cinnamon moderates holiday glucose

How to transition: Three days before solstice or equinox, introduce the new produce in a half-dose tonic. Let palate and digestion adapt. By Day 10 the seasonal version often tastes "right," and your body has fresh antioxidant allies.

Optional Paths — Fasting, Keto, and Your Mineral Bedrock

Intermittent Fasting (IF)

Mineral harmony makes IF easier: balanced sodium and magnesium dampen cortisol spikes that trigger false hunger. If you experiment with a 16:8 or 18:6 window:

1. **Keep the dawn tonic.** It contains < 20 calories; most pragmatic fasters allow it.
2. **Add a mid-fast salt crystal.** At hour ten, place one coarse grain on tongue; cravings fade in under a minute.

3. **Break fast with color + protein.** Aim for two hues and 25 g lean protein to prevent rebound binge.

Many readers report smoother adaptation and fewer headaches than traditional water-only fasts.

Keto or Low Carb

Sodium loss accelerates when insulin drops; electrolytes are non-negotiable.

- **Dawn tonic** increases to ⅓ tsp salt for the first two keto weeks.
- **Potassium guardrails**: avocado at least once daily, spinach or beet greens four cups weekly.
- **Magnesium rescue**: add 200 mg chelated magnesium glycinate at bedtime if leg cramps surface.

Stay attentive to thirst and blood pressure; adjust salt back down after "keto-flu" passes.

> *Remember:* your mineral ritual is the runway—fasting or keto is an optional aircraft. You can taxi, accelerate, or return to the gate without abandoning the solid asphalt beneath.

Reader Spotlights — One Year Later

Maya, 48 — The Consistency Maven

Maya kept the classic lemon tonic all year, cycling only her plate colors. Waist shrank six inches, HbA1c dropped from 5.9 to 5.3, and she now leads micro-burst breaks in her corporate office. Her secret: "Never let two red-icon days (missed micro-bursts) sit side by side on the calendar."

Jonas, 57 — The Late-Adopter Husband

Initially skeptical, Jonas sipped tonic "out of love" for his spouse. Six months later his GERD symptoms faded, and golf stamina soared. He embraced a 14:10 fasting window, still enjoys Saturday craft beer, and logs a perfect streak on the Gratitude Square—crediting mindset for his newfound patience with teenage sons.

Selene, 35 — The Perimenopause Trailblazer

Early hot flashes pushed Selene to a chilled mint-lime tonic, double magnesium foods, and Dream Stack devotion. One year on, flashes rare, cycle regularity improved, and she self-published a blog titled *Mineral Moon* chronicling the journey. Community badge "Lunar Guide" now bears her name.

These stories vary in age and lifestyle yet share one theme: adaptation without obsession. They tweaked dosage, flavor, or timing—but never abandoned the mineral anchor.

Staying Plugged In — Community, Challenges, and My Other Books

Quarterly Challenges

Every solstice and equinox a new 7-day micro-challenge drops in the hub:

- **Spring Clean:** add fermented color daily.
- **Summer Step-Up:** accrue 80 k steps per week.
- **Autumn Breath:** five breath ladders per day.
- **Winter Warmth:** nightly gratitude plus hot tonic variation.

Your Ongoing Mineral Manifesto

1. **Simple first.** Water, salt, citrus remain the cornerstone.
2. **Seasonal second.** Rotate produce with the calendar; let palate explore.
3. **Strategic third.** Add fasting, keto, or other protocols only when foundational habits feel effortless.
4. **Social always.** Share sunrise photos, laugh at mis-tossed salt mishaps, cheer another's badge. Humans heal in circles, not silos.

5. **Grace over grind.** Plateau? Illness? Vacation? Audit, adjust, resume—never punish.

Print these five lines; tape them inside the pantry door where the cookie bag used to tempt. Momentum is precious because it is fragile; protect it with reminders gentler than willpower.

A Dawn That Keeps Unfolding

The glass you lift tomorrow is not an ending but a beginning—again. Pink crystals swirl, lemon perfumes the air, warm water slips over tongue, and a message rushes through blood and nerve: *You are hydrated, resourced, safe to burn bright today.*

Let that message echo as seasons roll, projects swell, children grow, bones age, dreams pivot. Keep the mineral minute, color your plates, breathe, stretch, jot a nightly line of gratitude. Share the journey, tweak as needed, and return whenever life nudges you off-center. Sunrise will still be there, waiting to greet your glass with quiet gold.

Your Opinion Matters!

Thank You for Reading!

Dear Reader,

Thank you for taking the time to read my work. Sharing resourceful information and ideas with readers like you is one of the greatest joys of being an author.

If you found this book valuable, entertaining, or thought-provoking—or even if you have suggestions for improvement—I'd greatly appreciate your honest feedback in a review. Your thoughts not only help me grow but also guide other readers in discovering books they might enjoy or find useful.

Leaving a review is simple, and it makes a big difference. Thank you for your support—it truly means a lot!

With gratitude!

Eden Nora

Appendix A · Quick Ingredient Index

Below is a fast-scroll catalogue of every ingredient mentioned in the recipes and rituals, arranged in reader-friendly clusters so you can scan a farmers' market stall or grocery aisle and know exactly what to toss in the basket.

Mineral Staples

- **Pink Himalayan salt** – fine-grain for tonics, coarse for finishing plates.
- **Sea-salt travel sachets** – purse-sized insurance against restaurant undersalting.
- **Cream of tartar** – potassium powerhouse for Dream Stack tea or mid-afternoon resets.
- **Magnesium citrate powder** – emergency stir-in when travel heat or keto flushing strikes.

Dawn Citrus & Acids

- Lemons · Limes · Blood oranges · Ruby grapefruit
- Raw apple-cider vinegar (unfiltered, "mother" intact)

- Blackstrap molasses (iron and trace-mineral boost during menstruation)

Flavor Infusers

- Fresh herbs – mint, basil, rosemary, thyme, sage
- Roots & rhizomes – ginger knobs, turmeric fingers
- Spices – Ceylon cinnamon, smoked paprika, ground cardamom
- Floral notes – culinary lavender buds, rosewater drops

Protein Partners

- Wild salmon fillets, canned salmon with bones
- Hemp tofu blocks, tempeh for fermentation fans
- Pasture-raised eggs, chicken drumsticks (skin on for glycine)
- Collagen peptides or bone broth concentrate for grab-and-go glycine

Low-Glycemic Roots & Shoots

- Sweet potatoes (orange or purple) · Beets and beet greens
- Zucchini, bell peppers, broccolini, baby spinach
- Avocados for potassium rescue

Rainbow Antioxidant Extras

- Berries – blueberry, raspberry, strawberry, blackberry
- Watermelon chunks, pineapple tidbits, mango dice (summer cycling)
- Purple cabbage shreds, red-leaf lettuce, dark-leaf kale

Good-Fat Accents

- Cold-pressed olive oil for roasting and dressings
- Tahini, almond butter, avocado oil mayonnaise
- Mixed olives, toasted pumpkin seeds, dark-chocolate nibs

Keep this appendix dog-eared; a five-ingredient dinner becomes effortless when you can glance down, pair one protein, one root or shoot, one healthy fat, one herb or spice, and a citrus or acid accent.

APPENDIX B · PEER-REVIEWED REFERENCES

Chapter 1 – The One-Minute Mineral Switch

• Stachenfeld, N. "Sodium intake and its relation to hydration and performance," *Sports Science Review*, 2023.

• Gutiérrez-Macías, A. et al. "Electrolyte modulation of cortisol awakening response in perimenopausal women," *Journal of Endocrine Health*, 2022.

Chapter 2 – Electrolytes Whisper, Hormones Listen

• Williams, R.; Li, K. "Hydration status influences afternoon snack consumption," *Nutrients*, 2021.

• Gagnon, D. & Kenny, G. "Heat-stress, sweat sodium loss, and fluid replacement," *Physiology & Behavior*, 2024.

Chapter 3 – Twenty-One Sunrise Tonics

• Li, Z. et al. "Polyphenol-rich citrus infusions improve endothelial function," *Food Chemistry*, 2022.

• Borges, G. "Mint terpenes and digestive motility," *Phytotherapy Research*, 2020.

Chapter 4 – Real-Food Amplifiers

• Martínez-Steele, E. "Ultra-processed foods and mineral displacement," *Public Health Nutrition*, 2023.

• Kaczor, C. "Color diversity on the plate correlates with gut-microbiome richness," *Gut Microbes*, 2022.

Chapter 5 – Micro-Bursts & Lymph Flow

• Zawieja, D. "Mechanical stimulation of lymphatics during low-level activity," *Lymphatic Research*, 2021.

• Sander, H. "Three-minute movement breaks enhance cerebral blood flow," *Brain Imaging & Behavior*, 2024.

Chapter 6 – Mind Over Morning

• Peters, J.; Büchel, C. "Episodic future thinking reduces impulsive eating," *PNAS*, 2019.

• Benton, D. "Magnesium and sleep quality: a systematic review," *Nutrients*, 2022.

Chapter 7 – 14-Day Quick-Start

• Figueiredo, S. "Self-monitoring worksheets and habit adherence," *Behavioral Medicine*, 2020.

Chapter 8 – 28-Day Challenge

• Deci, E. & Ryan, R. "Community support and autonomous motivation," *Self-Determination Theory Handbook*, 2021.

Chapter 9 – Plateaus & Curveballs

• He, F. "Sodium-potassium balance and blood-pressure regulation across climates," *Hypertension*, 2023.

Chapter 10 – Future-Proofing Momentum

• Longo, V.; Anderson, D. "Intermittent fasting, vitamins, and mineral status," *Cell Metabolism*, 2024.

• Stubbs, B. "Seasonal produce variation and micronutrient intake," *Journal of Agricultural Science*, 2022.

These sources shaped the protocols and practical tips you've just completed. Scholarly updates will be posted twice a year on the book's resource page.

FREE Exclusive Health Bonus Pack

As a special thank you for picking up this book, you now have instant access to an *exclusive collection* of high-value digital tools, guides and **Videos — absolutely FREE** — designed to support your weight loss journey and overall health beyond the pages.

Download instantly at https://mayobook.com/weightloss-bonus or scan the QR code below!

https://mayobook.com/weightloss-bonus

Here's What You'll Get When You Download the Bonus Pack:

1. Keto Recipe Video Vault

Professional, High-Quality Cooking Videos to Inspire & Monetize

Step inside the booming world of keto content with a curated collection of ready-to-use recipe videos — perfect for your personal use.

Each video is crafted to be visually captivating and informative.

What makes it special:

- HD-quality and ready-to-use
- Perfect for everyone
- Stay ahead of trends with in-demand recipes that people are searching for
- Use them to **inspire meals**, or **educate yourself.**

2. Easy Keto: Your Complete Beginner's Blueprint

Learn the "why" behind the keto lifestyle and how to master it for life.

This is more than a crash course. It's a full guide to help you understand how the keto diet works — and how to actually stick with it. Whether you're brand-new or burned out by fad diets, this guide will reshape how you think about food, energy, and weight.

Inside you'll discover:

- Why keto works (even when other diets fail)

- The science behind burning fat instead of sugar
- The truth about ketosis, macros, and energy crashes
- What to eat, what to avoid, and how to plan meals with ease
- Delicious recipe ideas to stay on track and never feel deprived

3. Boost Your Immune System: A Natural Healing Guide

Because a strong body starts with a resilient defense system.

Weight loss isn't just about looking better — it's about feeling better, too. This powerful resource gives you the natural tools to support your immune system while reducing stress and inflammation.

What you'll gain:

- A clear understanding of how your immune system functions
- Daily habits and immune-boosting foods that make a real difference
- Simple stress relief tips for a healthier mind and body
- The best essential oils and how to use them safely for immunity

4. Carb Cycling for Weight Loss & Hormone Harmony

A powerful fat-loss method trusted by athletes and now tailored for women.

If you've hit a plateau or need a reset strategy, this guide is your next step. Carb cycling allows you to enjoy flexibility without compromising results. It's the missing link for women dealing with stubborn fat, slow metabolism, or hormone imbalances.

What this guide will teach you:

- The basics of carb cycling and why it works so well
- Key differences between keto and carb cycling
- How to plan your high-carb and low-carb days
- Fat-burning meal ideas that support muscle tone and energy
- A sustainable strategy that supports long-term success

Unlock All 4 Bonuses Instantly

All bonuses are delivered digitally and are yours to keep forever. Just visit the link or scan the QR code included inside the book to start downloading:

https://mayobook.com/weightloss-bonus
Or scan the QR code above for instant access

Why Are These Bonuses Free?

Because *you matter.*
Because you're not just buying a book — you're investing in your future.
And because we want you to succeed far beyond these pages.

These tools are designed to complement your journey and make weight loss *feel doable*, *enjoyable*, and *sustainable* — no matter your age or starting point.

Don't Miss Out

Tens of thousands of readers have already downloaded their bonus pack — and many say it's what helped them finally stay consistent and see results.

Now it's your turn.
Get your exclusive Health Bonus Pack today and take your transformation to the next level.

Acknowledgements

A book is a sunrise watched by many eyes. Mine simply caught the first glimmer.

To Dr. Marissa Chen—thank you for lending clinical authority and a generous heart to the foreword, and for challenging me to translate endocrinology into plain comfort.

To the beta-reader circle—Amara J., Jonas K., Selene P., Maya R.—your weekly voice memos, recipe tweaks, and honest "this part still feels fuzzy" notes lifted the manuscript from helpful to human.

To the nutrition science librarians —your patience while I chased down odd corner journals turned anecdote into evidence.

To my family, especially the ever-patient teenagers—thank you for tolerating kitchen counters permanently dusted in salt crystals and for rating every sunrise tonic, even the beet one.

And finally, **to you, the reader**—for opening these pages, stirring that first glass, and trusting your own body enough to let it speak. May your mornings stay mineral-bright, and may we meet again in my next book, or in the quiet companionship of another shared sunrise.

— *Eden Nora*

About the Author

Eden Nora stands as a luminary in the realm of health and wellness, captivating audiences with her profound insights and transformative guidance. With an impressive track record that spans over two decades, Eden Nora has dedicated her life to empowering individuals on their journey to optimal health, drawing deeply from her rich personal experiences and rigorous research.

Born and raised in a multicultural household, Eden developed an early appreciation for diverse health practices. This unique upbringing ignited her passion for understanding holistic well-being, inspiring her to pursue advanced studies in nutrition, psychology, and integrative medicine. Her academic prowess is matched by her hands-on experience, having worked with leading health institutions globally, where she honed her expertise in crafting personalized health strategies.

Eden's compelling narrative is woven with stories of resilience and transformation. A survivor of a chronic health condition herself, she intimately understands the challenges her readers face. This personal journey fuels her commitment to demystifying health concepts and offering practical, sustainable solutions. Her approach is anchored in empathy and evidence-based research, resonating deeply with a diverse audience seeking authentic and actionable health advice.

Eden Nora's writings are a testament to her belief in the interconnection between mind, body, and spirit. Her bestselling books and articles have garnered a loyal readership, consistently praised for their clarity, depth, and accessibility. Her nuanced perspective blends traditional wisdom with modern science, making her a trusted voice in health and wellness circles.

As a sought-after speaker and consultant, Eden's influence extends beyond the written word. She regularly collaborates with wellness brands and thought leaders, contributing to innovative projects that shape the future of health and wellness. Her work is not only transformative but also inclusive, catering to a demography that values diversity, authenticity, and empowerment.

Eden Nora's authoritative presence in the health and wellness industry is a beacon for those seeking to enhance their well-being. Her dedication to fostering a healthier world is unwavering, and her ability to inspire change is unparalleled. For those on a quest for holistic health, Eden Nora is an indispensable guide, offering wisdom and encouragement every step of the way.

Printed in Dunstable, United Kingdom

65937328R00067